The Life and Work of...
Michelangelo Buonarroti

Richard Tames

Heinemann Library
Chicago, Illinois

© 2001 Reed Educational & Professional Publishing
Published by Heinemann Library,
an imprint of Reed Educational & Professional Publishing,
Chicago, IL

Customer Service 1-888-454-2279

Visit our website at www.heinemannlibrary.com

Designed by Celia Floyd
Illustrations by Sam Thompson
Originated by Dot Gradations
Printed in Hong Kong/China

05 04 03 02 01
10 9 8 7 6 5 4 3 2 1

Library of Congress Cataloging-in-Publication Data
Tames, Richard.
    Michelangelo Buonarotti / Richard Tames.
      p. cm. – (The Life and work of--)
    Includes bibliographical references and index.
    Summary: A biography of the Renaissance sculptor, painter, architect, and poet,
including a list of places where his art can be seen today.
    ISBN 1-57572-343-3 (lib. bdg.)   ISBN 1-58810-289-0 (pbk. bdg.)
    1. Michelangelo Buonarotti, 1475-1564—Juvenile literature. 2.
Artists—Italy—Biography—Juvenile literature. [1. Michelangelo Buonarotti, 1475-1564.
2. Artists.] I. Title. II. Series.

N6923.B9 T36 2000
709'.2—dc21
[B]   00-025785

Acknowledgments
The Publishers would like to thank the following for permission to reproduce photographs:

Archivi Alinari, pp. 5, 9, 11, 13, 15, 21; Archivio Buonarroti, p. 27; Bridgeman Art Library/Casa Buonarroti, Florence, p. 7; Bridgeman Art Library/Vatican Museums and Galleries, Italy, p. 17; E. T. Archive, p. 28; J. Allan Cash, Ltd., p. 23; Photo RMN/R. G. Ojeda, p. 19; Robert Harding Picture Library/Simon Harris, p. 25; Scala, Museo dellí Opera del Duomo, p. 29

Cover photograph reproduced with permission of The Bridgeman Art Library

Every effort has been made to contact copyright holders of any material reproduced in this book. Any omissions will be rectified in subsequent printings if notice is given to the Publisher.

Some words in this book are in bold, **like this.** You can find out what they mean by looking in the glossary.

Contents

Who Was Michelangelo? 4

The Pupil 6

The Student 8

Fame 10

Working in Florence 12

The Pope's Tomb 14

The Sistine Chapel 16

Cities at War 18

Working for the Medici 20

Back to Rome 22

The Pope's Architect 24

Last Years 26

Michelangelo Dies 28

Timeline 30

Glossary 31

More Books to Read 31

More Artwork to See 31

Index 32

Who Was Michelangelo?

Michelangelo was one of the greatest artists of all time. He lived during the **Renaissance**. He thought of himself as a **sculptor**. But he was also a painter, a poet, and an **architect**.

In Michelangelo's time, most art was made for churches. This painting shows God giving life to Adam. Michelangelo painted it on the ceiling of the Sistine **Chapel** in Rome, Italy.

The Pupil

Michelangelo was born in Italy on March 6, 1475. As a boy, he studied painting with Ghirlandaio, a respected artist. Later, he studied artworks owned by an important, powerful family—the Medici.

Soon Michelangelo became interested in **sculpture** as well as painting. He was only sixteen when he carved this sculpture of the baby Jesus with his mother, Mary.

The Student

Michelangelo wanted to understand how the human body worked. He studied human bodies in a hospital in a city called Florence. This helped him make his paintings and **sculptures** look real.

Michelangelo also studied the work of other artists. He made his own drawings of **frescoes** like this one, by Masaccio. This helped him learn about color and **perspective**.

Fame

Michelangelo moved to the city of Rome in 1496. There, he carved a famous **statue**. It shows Jesus lying in his mother's arms after he has died.

The statue is called the *Pietà*. Michelangelo used one piece of stone to make the two figures. It is very **realistic**. You can see the folds in the cloth of Mary's dress.

Working in Florence

In 1501, Michelangelo returned to Florence. He had been asked to make a **statue** of **David.** David was a hero and a leader. His life is described in the **Bible.**

Michelangelo's statue of David was for the city's **cathedral**. The statue became famous. People thought it showed a perfect human being.

The Pope's Tomb

In 1505, Michelangelo was asked to plan a huge **tomb**. It would be for **Pope** Julius II. But Michelangelo had agreed to do too much work. He did not have time to finish the tomb.

Over 40 **statues** were planned for the tomb.
This famous statue of **Moses** was meant to be
on the tomb.

The Sistine Chapel

In 1508, **Pope** Julius II gave Michelangelo a special job. He asked Michelangelo to paint works of art. They would be painted on the ceiling of the Sistine **Chapel** in Rome.

It took Michelangelo four years to paint the ceiling. The paintings tell stories from the **Bible**. They are among the most famous paintings in the world.

Cities at War

Italy was often at war during Michelangelo's lifetime. Between 1528 and 1529, he worked on plans for buildings and walls to protect Florence during an attack.

Michelangelo made this sketch in 1528. It shows his plans for the **defense** of Florence. He wanted ditches dug all around the city.

Working for the Medici

From 1515 until 1534, Michelangelo worked for the Medici family in Florence. He **designed** a **chapel**, a library, two **tombs,** and a grand house for them.

This is a tomb Michelangelo designed for the Medici family. The two figures at the front are meant to be Dawn and **Dusk**.

Back to Rome

From 1534 until he died, Michelangelo lived in Rome. He **designed** a new square for the center of the city.

Michelangelo redesigned the old city hall on Capitolene Hill. He also created a floor design of oval patterns. He had a **statue** placed at the center of the pattern.

The Pope's Architect

In 1546, Michelangelo became the **pope's** main **architect**. He worked on the great church of St. Peter in Rome.

Michelangelo **designed** the **dome** of St. Peter's. Sadly, he died before it was finished.

Last Years

From 1546 to 1547, Michelangelo **designed** a palace. It was for **Pope** Paul III's family. He also wrote many poems and letters to his friends and family.

Michelangelo had beautiful handwriting. Many of his poems are about love. But he never married.

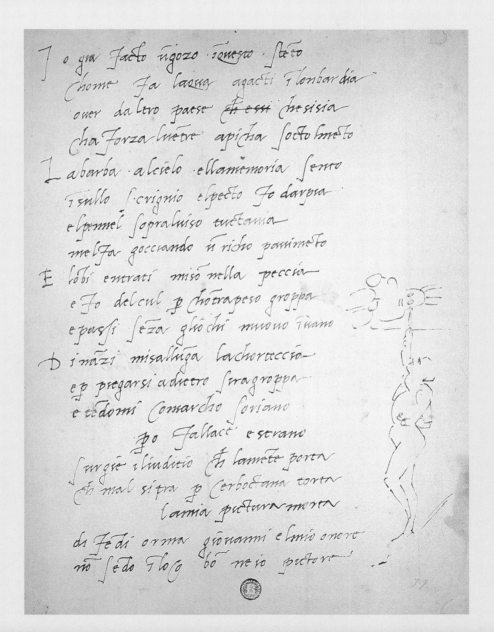

Michelangelo Dies

Michelangelo died on February 18, 1564. He was 88 years old. He was buried in Florence. His **tomb** was designed by one of his students, Giorgio Vasari.

This is part of a **statue** Michelangelo was making
for his own tomb. But he never finished it.
It shows Michelangelo at the age of 75.

Timeline

1475	Michelangelo Buonarroti born in Caprese, Italy on March 6
1475	Family moves to Florence
1488	Trains with the artist Ghirlandaio
1490–1492	Lives in the Medici Palace and studies art
1496	Moves from Florence to Rome
1501–1504	Carves **statue** of **David**
1508–1512	Paints ceiling of Sistine **Chapel**
1528–1529	**Designs defenses** for Florence
1534	Last time Michelangelo leaves Florence
1534–1541	Michelangelo paints **fresco** *(The Last Judgment)* for Sistine Chapel
1546	Michelangelo becomes pope's chief **architect**
1564	Michelangelo dies, February 18

Glossary

architect   person who designs buildings

Bible   book of Christian holy writings, divided into the Old and the New Testaments

biography   story of a person's life

cathedral   large and important church

chapel   small church or part of a bigger church or cathedral

David   hero of the Old Testament and later King of Israel

defense   something built to keep a city safe

design   to make a plan

dome   rounded roof

dusk   evening

fresco   painting done on wet plaster so the color soaks in

Moses   Old Testament leader to whom God gave the Ten Commandments

perspective   way of drawing to show distance

pope   leader of the Roman Catholic Church

realistic   lifelike

Renaissance   the fourteenth through the seventeenth centuries in Europe, when there was great new interest in art and learning

sculptor   person who makes statues or carvings

sculpture   statue or carving

statue   carved, molded, or sculptured figure

tomb   burial place

More Books to Read

McLanathan, Richard B. *Michelangelo.* New York, Harry N. Abrams, Inc., 1993.

Venezia, Mike. *Michelangelo.* Danbury, Conn.: Children's Press, 1991.

More Artwork to See

Drawing for the *Libyan Sybil*, Metropolitan Museum of Art, New York, New York

Drawing for the *Holy Family with the Infant John the Baptist,* Getty Museum, Los Angeles, California

Index

birth   6
death   28
Medici family   6, 20, 21
paintings
    Creation of Adam, Sistine
Chapel   5
    Sistine Chapel ceiling   17
Pope Julius II   14, 16
Pope Paul III   24, 26
St. Peter's   24, 25
sculpture
    statue of *David*   12, 13
    Madonna of the Stairs   7

sculpture (continued)
    statue of *Moses*   15
    the *Pietà*   11
    self portrait   29
Sistine Chapel   5, 16, 17
tombs
    of Lorenzo d'Medici   21
    of Michelangelo   28
    of Pope Julius II   14, 15
Trinita, by Masaccio   9
war   18, 19